BOOKWORMS

Creepy Crawlers

Wasps

Jack K. Patterson

Cavendish Square
New York

Published in 2019 by Cavendish Square Publishing, LLC
243 5th Avenue, Suite 136, New York, NY 10016

First Edition

Library of Congress Cataloging-in-Publication Data

Names: Patterson, Jack K., 1988- author.
Title: Wasps / Jack K. Patterson.
Description: First edition. | New York : Cavendish Square, 2019. | Series: Creepy crawlers |
Audience: Grades K-3. | Includes bibliographical references and index.
Identifiers: LCCN 2018024816 (print) | LCCN 2018025901 (ebook) | ISBN 9781502643001 (ebook) |
ISBN 9781502642714 (library bound) | ISBN 9781502642981 (pbk.) | ISBN 9781502642998 (6 pack)
Subjects: LCSH: Wasps--Juvenile literature.
Classification: LCC SB945.W3 (ebook) | LCC SB945.W3 P38 2019 (print) | DDC 595.79--dc23
LC record available at https://lccn.loc.gov/2018024816

Editorial Director: David McNamara
Editor: Kristen Susienka
Copy Editor: Nathan Heidelberger
Associate Art Director: Alan Sliwinski
Designer: Megan Metté
Production Coordinator: Karol Szymczuk
Photo Research: J8 Media

The photographs in this book are used by permission and through the courtesy of: Cover RomBo 64/Shutterstock,com; p. 5 Ruth Swan/Shutterstock.com; p. 7 Nataba/iStockphoto.com; p. 9 Lynn H. Armstrong photography/Moment/Getty Images; p. 11 Adrienne Bresnahan/Moment/Getty Images; p. 13 Blickwinkel/ Alamy Stock Photo; p. 15 Perennou Nuridsany/Science Source; p. 17 Geza Farkas/Shutterstock.com; p. 19 Kim Takhyzsviridov/Shutterstock.com; p. 21 Irina Kozorog/Shutterstock.com.

Printed in the United States of America

Contents

Wasps look a little creepy.

They look like bees.

But they are not bees.

Wasps are yellow and black.

They have wings.

Female wasps have
a sharp point.

It is called a stinger.

Wasps start life inside an egg.

The egg is in a nest.

Young wasps are called **larvae** and **pupae**.

They grow into adult wasps.

Most wasps live in a **colony**.

Every wasp has a job.

Female wasps are
called workers.

Male wasps are
called drones.

Only one wasp is the queen.

The workers and drones are the queen's children.

One day, other queen wasps will be born.

They will start new colonies.

Wasps like warm weather.

They also like to drink
from flowers or leaves.

Sometimes they eat
other insects.

Wasps help keep flowers growing.

They do this by **pollinating**.

Watch out!

A female wasp will sting you if you bother her.

Have you seen a wasp near you?

New Words

colony (KAH-low-nee) Many wasps living together.

larvae (LAR-vay) Baby wasps that have just left their eggs.

pollinating (POLL-in-AY-ting) When bees and wasps go from flower to flower, taking part of each flower to other flowers.

pupae (PEW-pay) Wasps that are not yet adults.

Index

About the Author

Jack K. Patterson lives in Boston, Massachusetts. He enjoys gardening, bird watching, and exploring the outdoors. He is an insect enthusiast who has his own bug collection. He enjoys learning about the world around him.

About BOOKWORMS

Bookworms help independent readers gain reading confidence through high-frequency words, simple sentences, and strong picture/text support. Each book explores a concept that helps children relate what they read to the world they live in.